EXPLORE BIOMES

MARINE BIOMES

BY CECILIA PINTO McCARTHY

Kids Core
An Imprint of Abdo Publishing
abdobooks.com

abdobooks.com

Published by Abdo Publishing, a division of ABDO, PO Box 398166, Minneapolis, Minnesota 55439.

Printed in the United States of America, North Mankato, Minnesota.
052023
092023

THIS BOOK CONTAINS RECYCLED MATERIALS

Cover Photo: iStockphoto
Interior Photos: Magnus Larsson/iStockphoto, 4–5; Dirscherl Reinhard/Prisma/SuperStock, 6; Jeffrey Rotman/Science Source, 8; Imagine Earth Photography/Shutterstock Images, 10–11; Alejo Miranda/Shutterstock Images, 13; Marko Steffensen/Alamy, 14; Irina Markova/Shutterstock Images, 17; Kochneva Tetyana/Shutterstock Images, 18; Shutterstock Images, 20–21, 25, 26, 28 (seaweed), 28–29; Isabelle Kuehn/Shutterstock Images, 23; Nadya Art/Shutterstock Images, 28 (clown fish, turtle), 29 (shark, seahorse, crab)

Editor: Angela Lim
Series Designer: Ryan Gale

Library of Congress Control Number: 2022949098

Publisher's Cataloging-in-Publication Data

Names: McCarthy, Cecilia Pinto, author.
Title: Marine Biomes / by Cecilia Pinto McCarthy
Description: Minneapolis, Minnesota: Abdo Publishing Company, 2024 | Series: Explore biomes | Includes online resources and index.
Identifiers: ISBN 9781098291112 (lib. bdg.) | ISBN 9781098277291 (ebook)
Subjects: LCSH: Ocean--Juvenile literature. | Biotic communities--Juvenile literature. | Habitats--Juvenile literature. | Life zones--Juvenile literature. | Marine animals--Juvenile literature. | Marine plants--Juvenile literature. | Marine ecology--Juvenile literature.
Classification: DDC 577--dc23

CONTENTS

Clown fish live in coral reefs. They can be found off the coasts of Australia and Asia.

CHAPTER 1

LIVING ON A REEF

A clown fish swims among a sea anemone's tentacles. Sea anemones live in coral reefs. Their tentacles have stingers that are deadly to some animals. But the clown fish is not in danger. Its scales have a slimy coating that protects it from being stung.

More than 1 million animal species live in marine biomes.

A shark swims overhead. The clown fish hides in the tentacles. After the danger has passed, the clown fish helps the anemone. Its movements keep the anemone clean. As it swims, the clown fish causes **nutrients** to flow across the anemone's tentacles.

What Is a Biome?

Earth is made up of natural areas called biomes. Each biome includes plants, animals, and nonliving things. Plants in marine biomes include seagrass and kelp. Clown fish and sea anemones are marine animals. Nonliving things include sand and rocks. Water temperature and depth determine the plants and animals found in marine biomes.

Marine biomes contain salt water. Most of the salt comes from rocks on land. Rain breaks down rocks into smaller pieces.

More to Explore

Marine biomes are in the ocean. More than 80 percent of the ocean is unexplored. It is challenging to study the deep ocean. There is no sunlight. The water can be very cold. In some areas, underwater volcanoes spew water that is more than 700 degrees Fahrenheit (370°C).

Scientists use submarines to explore the deep ocean.

Salts from the rocks wash into rivers. The rivers carry the salts to the ocean.

Marine biomes keep Earth warm. They absorb heat from the sun. Ocean **currents** move warm water around the globe. Living things in the ocean make more than half of the oxygen on Earth. In this way, marine biomes help life on land.

PRIMARY SOURCE

José Pablo Murillo is a program manager for the Stockholm International Water Institute. He described why the world needs healthy oceans:

> The importance of healthy oceans cannot be overestimated: 80 percent of all life on Earth can be found in the oceans. They provide food [and] employment.

Source: José Pablo Murillo. "Valuing Water from Source to Sea." *SIWI*, 23 Mar. 2021, siwi.org. Accessed 30 Sept. 2022.

What's the Big Idea?

Read this quote carefully. What is its main idea? Explain how the main idea is supported by details.

Animals such as the humpback whale travel great distances in the ocean.

CHAPTER 2

HOW MARINE BIOMES FORM

Billions of years ago, there was no liquid water on Earth. Volcanoes gave off steam. The steam became clouds as Earth cooled. **Precipitation** fell from the clouds and filled low-lying areas on Earth. Marine biomes formed over millions of years.

There are three types of marine biomes. These are oceans, coral reefs, and estuaries. Together, they cover three-quarters of the planet.

Oceans

Oceans are the largest biome on Earth. Earth has five oceans, which are connected. They are the Atlantic, Pacific, Indian, Arctic, and Southern Oceans. Ocean water is warmer near the **equator**. It is colder close to the North and South Poles.

Oceans can be divided into layers called zones. The sunlight zone extends from the ocean's surface to approximately 655 feet (200 m) underwater. This zone is the warmest.

Ocean Zones

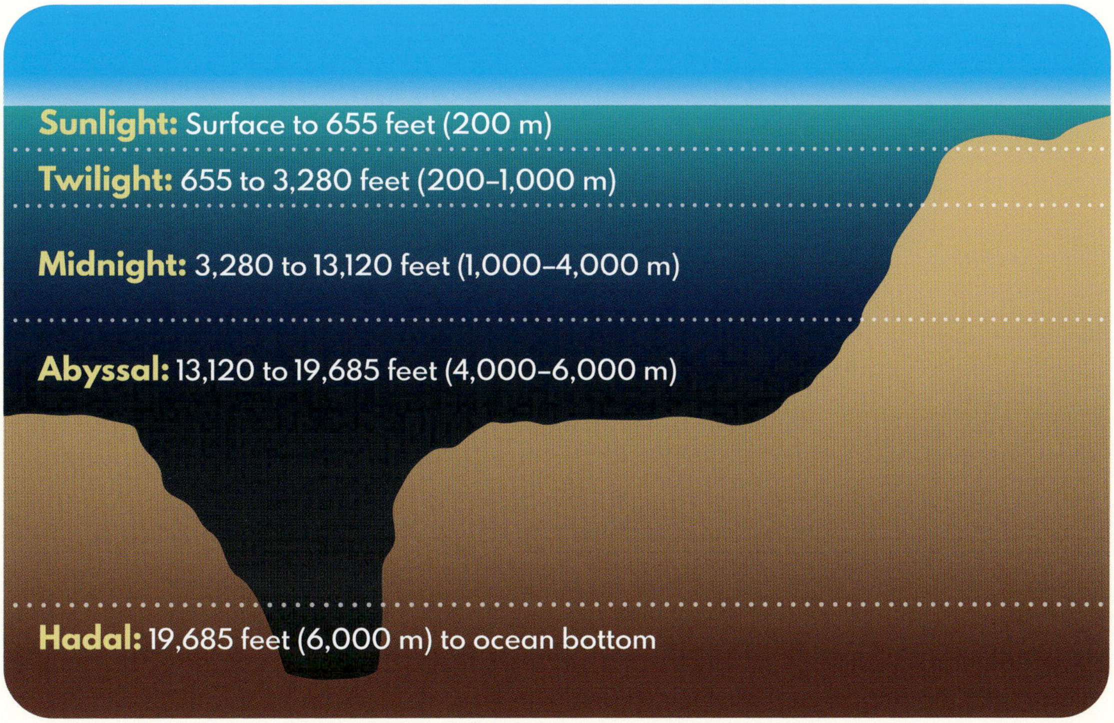

Each ocean zone has different amounts of light and different temperatures. Certain animals live within each zone.

It receives the most sunlight. The next zone is the twilight zone. It goes to 3,280 feet (1,000 m) below the surface. A small amount of sunlight enters the twilight zone. Most marine plants and animals live in the sunlight and twilight zones.

The deep-sea anglerfish lives in the midnight zone.

The midnight, abyssal, and hadal zones make up the deep ocean. No sunlight enters these zones. The water is extremely cold. These conditions make it difficult for many living things to survive.

Coral Reefs

Coral reefs are made up of corals. Each coral is made up of tiny marine animals called polyps. Polyps are very sensitive. They need sunlight and clean water. Most can survive only in water temperatures between 73 and 84 degrees Fahrenheit (23–29°C).

Coral Bleaching

Special **algae** live within coral polyps. Algae and corals keep each other healthy. Algae give corals their color. But corals sometimes expel algae when stressed. The corals become white. This is known as coral bleaching. Pollution and high temperatures can lead to coral bleaching. Bleached corals often die.

Reefs have hard and soft corals. Hard corals form the foundation for reefs. Polyps attach to hard surfaces, such as rocks. They produce skeletons. The skeletons protect the soft bodies of the corals. New polyps grow on top of old skeletons.

Soft corals do not produce skeletons. They look like fans or trees. Soft corals can be found in reefs. But because they do not have skeletons, they do not form reefs like hard corals do. Approximately 400 types of soft and hard corals live in the Great Barrier Reef near Australia. It is the largest coral reef in the world.

Most coral reefs are between 5,000 and 10,000 years old.

Hardangerfjord is a fjord in Norway. It connects to the Atlantic Ocean.

Estuaries

An estuary forms where a river or stream meets an ocean or sea. Estuaries have a mixture of fresh and salt water. Some estuaries are partially enclosed by reefs or long, thin islands near a coast.

Fjords are a type of estuary. They are formed by **glaciers**. Some glaciers flow toward the ocean. They create narrow channels along the coast. Ocean water mixes with fresh water from the melting glaciers.

Explore Online

Visit the website below. Does it give any new information about coral reefs that wasn't in Chapter Two?

Coral Reef Facts

abdocorelibrary.com/marine-biomes

Most plankton are too small to see without a microscope.

CHAPTER 3

LIFE IN MARINE BIOMES

Many animals live in marine biomes. Some swim in the open ocean. Others are found closer to shore. Different living things are found at different depths.

Plankton drift in ocean currents. Some plankton are plantlike. Others are tiny animals.

Plankton are vital to the marine biome. Some produce oxygen. Many animals eat plankton.

Ocean animals come in many sizes. Krill are a type of plankton. They look like tiny shrimp. Krill are the main food source of blue whales, the largest animals in the world. Blue whales can weigh up to 200 tons (181 metric tons).

Some marine animals are found only in certain zones. Water in the sunlight zone is warm. This zone is rich in plant and animal life. Green sea turtles live in the sunlight zone. The females come onshore to lay eggs.

Other marine animals spend their time in the deep ocean. Food is harder to find where sunlight does not reach. But the darkness also helps animals hide from **predators**.

Green sea turtles are herbivores. They eat seagrasses and algae.

Deep-sea anglerfish live in the midnight zone. These fish have a spine that dangles above their mouths. The spine glows. It attracts small animals to eat.

Some marine animals travel between ocean zones. Lantern fish spend their days in the twilight zone. They travel to the surface at night to feed. At night, it is harder for predators to see the feeding lantern fish.

Underwater Nurseries

Estuaries and coral reefs are nurseries for marine animals. Mangrove trees grow in

Plastic Pollution

More than 14 million tons (12.7 million metric tons) of plastic ends up in the ocean every year. Plastics harm and kill marine animals. Animals can get tangled in plastic ropes, bags, and other items. Sea turtles, seabirds, fish, and whales may die after eating plastic they mistake for food.

Many fish species shelter among the roots of mangrove trees.

some estuaries. The trees can grow in fresh or salt water. They can also survive changes in water levels. They have curved roots that form safe habitats for young fish. The roots keep out large predators. The Atlantic goliath grouper spends the first years of its life near mangroves. The young fish hide in and feed on the leaf litter.

Coral reefs also shelter young fish. Reefs have many spaces where fish can hide.

Seahorses rely on coral reefs. They wrap their tails around corals when they sleep and eat to avoid being swept out to the open ocean.

There is plenty of food to help young animals grow. Some sharks rely on coral reefs for food and shelter. The white spotted bamboo shark lays its eggs in coral reefs. Each egg has a long tendril that wraps around corals. This prevents the egg from drifting into the open ocean.

Marine biomes are rich with plant and animal life. These biomes also provide oxygen, food, and other resources for people. But marine biomes face many threats. Pollution harms these biomes. Overfishing reduces populations of fish and other animals. It is important to protect these natural areas and the plants and animals that live there.

Further Evidence

Look at the website below. Does it give any information about marine biomes that wasn't in Chapter Three?

Ocean Habitat

abdocorelibrary.com/marine-biomes

EXPLORE THE BIOME

Many plants and animals help make up marine biomes. Can you identify which parts of this marine biome are plants? Which are animals? Can you find any nonliving parts of the biome?

Glossary

algae
plant or plantlike living things that commonly live in water

currents
the flow or movements of water

equator
the imaginary circle that goes around Earth halfway between the North and South Poles

glaciers
large bodies of snow and ice that move across land

nutrients
materials that living things need in order to grow and stay alive

precipitation
liquid or frozen water that falls from the sky, including rain, sleet, and snow

predators
animals that hunt other animals for food

Online Resources

To learn more about marine biomes, visit our free resource websites below.

Core Library CONNECTION
FREE! COMMON CORE MULTIMEDIA RESOURCES

Visit **abdocorelibrary.com** or scan this QR code for free Common Core resources for teachers and students, including vetted activities, multimedia, and booklinks, for deeper subject comprehension.

Booklinks NONFICTION NETWORK
FREE! ONLINE NONFICTION RESOURCES

Visit **abdobooklinks.com** or scan this QR code for free additional online weblinks for further learning. These links are routinely monitored and updated to provide the most current information available.

Learn More

Beer, Julie, and Michelle Harris. *Weird but True! Ocean: 300 Fin-tastic Facts from the Deep Blue Sea*. National Geographic, 2021.

French, Jess. *Earth's Incredible Oceans*. DK, 2021.

Index

About the Author

Cecilia Pinto McCarthy enjoys sharing her love of nature with young readers. When she is not writing, she teaches at a nature center. She lives north of Boston, Massachusetts.